Explore
Music
through
Word Games

*David Wheway and
Shelagh Thomson*

18 varied national curriculum
Music activities linked to the
English attainment targets

Music Department
OXFORD UNIVERSITY PRESS
Oxford and New York

Oxford University Press, Walton Street, Oxford OX2 6DP, England

Oxford is a trade mark of Oxford University Press

© David Wheway and Shelagh Thomson, 1993

With the exception of the line drawings which may be reproduced for non-commercial use within the classroom, no part of this publication may be reproduced, stored in a retrieval system, or transmitted in any form or by any means, electronic, mechanical, photocopying, recording, or otherwise, without the prior permission of the Publishers.

First published 1993
ISBN 0 19 321869 0
Design and illustration by Creative Intelligence, Bristol
Printed in Great Britain by Caligraving Ltd., Thetford, Norfolk

Contents

4	**Introduction**
	List of Activities
8	Treasure Chest
9	Boo!
10	Colouring Names
11	Ants
12	Creepy Crawlies
13	Connect
14	Associations
15	Name Tunes
16	Sound Chance
17	Syllabox
18	Music Critic
20	Moving Words
21	Word Tunes
22	Pitch Words
23	Pitch Sentences
24	Voices Galore
25	Thesaurus
26	Crack the Clue
	Appendix
27	Glossary
28	Pentatonic Scales

There are nine books in this series:
Explore Music through
 Art, Geography, History, Maths, Movement,
 Poetry and Rhyme, Science, Stories, Word Games.

Introduction

These booklets are designed for primary teachers who value the role of music in an integrated approach to the curriculum. They are of equal value to those who have little or no experience of teaching music, or those who have responsibility as a music co-ordinator.

By closely relating musical activities to other areas of the curriculum, it is hoped that primary teachers will feel more confident when engaging in musical activities with children.

Within each of the nine booklets in the series, activities are ordered progressively from 'early years' through to upper Key Stage 2.

The appropriateness of any activity will depend on the previous experience of the child or group. For this reason we have not recommended any activity for a specific age group, but have indicated a target Key Stage.

Many activities, especially those primarily concerned with composition, are often best delivered over a number of sessions. This allows time for exploratory work, and also for evaluation, discussion, and development.

Building a Repertoire of Sounds

Children need an ever-increasing knowledge of sounds, and teachers need to be aware of the importance of sound exploration for future musical activities. This repertoire of sounds is especially important when children wish to represent feelings, objects, and other sounds in their compositions.

Body and Vocal Sounds

Children should explore the possibility for sounds made both vocally and with the body. For instance, how many sounds can be made with the throat? ('Ooooh', 'Ahhhh', a hiccup, a cough, a gargle, humming, sighing, panting, etc.) What different sounds can be made by patting different parts of the body? (Cheeks, chest, stomach, thighs, knees, etc.)

Classroom Percussion

Children should be encouraged to find as many different ways as possible to play percussion. Can it be scraped, tapped, shaken, scratched, blown, etc.? When a new sound is found, think about what moods or images it conjures up. Such exploration works well in small groups, using a limited number of instruments. Allow the children time to play new sounds to the rest of the class.

Percussion Resources

Some considerations when building resources:

Do your percussion resources offer a wide choice for creating a variety of sounds?

Are the instruments made from a variety of materials (e.g. wood, metal, plastic, etc.)?

Does the collection contain instruments from different ethnic origins?

Are the instruments of good quality? Remember, as in other areas of the curriculum, poor quality materials (e.g. worn or broken) may lead to poor or disappointing results.

Other Sound Makers

A wide variety of sounds can be made with everyday objects such as paper, kitchen utensils, beads and pulses (e.g. paper tearing, scrunching, flapping; pulses poured into a bucket, swirled around, shaken; pots and pans drum-kit).

When performing any activity, try different combinations of sound, as this adds to the children's exploratory work, and their understanding of timbre and texture.

Recording

It is very important that children develop ways of recording their compositions. A variety of ways are suggested throughout the booklets, for example, pictures, symbols, words, letters, and so on. Ensure paper and appropriate recording materials are always available.

Audio as well as video recorders are also valuable resources for recording children's work and development.

The Activities

Suggested Materials

These materials should be useful as a guide for preparing the lessons. They are only suggestions and teachers may wish to select their own materials.

Suggested Listening

Generally, it is a good idea to keep extracts short, e.g. 30–60 seconds in duration. If possible, tape-record extracts beforehand to avoid searching in the lesson.

Most of the suggestions given are easily available in record libraries or through record shops. Many can be found on compilations. Where this is not the case, a reference is given.

The recordings we have recommended should not be considered either obligatory or comprehensive.

Personal collections of recorded music are a valuable resource. However, do avoid limiting the children's listening opportunities to any one type of music.

Attainment Target Boxes

The left-hand box gives an indication of the main focus of each activity, relating to the national curriculum for Music. However it should be noted that the activities will also offer a variety of other musical experiences.

The right-hand box indicates how the activity may complement work undertaken in another area of the curriculum.

Classroom Organization

For many whole-class activities, a circle of children on a carpet or chairs is ideal. This helps concentration and promotes a feeling of involvement, as well as being practical when it comes to observing other children, whole-group involvement, and passing games. It might be advisable at times to split the class or set into groups.

There are some activities that require little or no percussion, and if you are just starting out you may feel more confident attempting these activities initially.

Handing Out Instruments

Avoid the children making a headlong rush to the music trolley at all costs! Allow the children to collect, or hand out, a few instruments at a time.

- Have the required instruments placed out ready beforehand.
- While listening to instructions, children should place their instruments on the floor in front of them.
- Give out beaters for instruments last.

- Before commencing agree on clear signals for stopping and putting instruments down (e.g. a hand in the air, a finger to the lips, a wink of the eye, etc.).
- Demand an immediate response to these signals.
- Encourage children to treat instruments with respect at all times. (This is not easy if instruments are worn or broken.)

Evaluation and Appraisal

When children are working on a composition, there should be regular evaluation by the teacher, and/or by the children, of how the work is progressing. This will include a great deal of purposeful listening and appraising. The process will in turn help the children in appraising the music of others.

Key Questions for Performers and Audience

Can you tell us about your music?

How did the piece start/finish?

What did you like about it?

What contrasts/changes did the piece contain?

Does the piece fulfil the task set?

Was it performed fluently and appropriately?

Could it have been improved, and if so, how?

Could the piece be extended, and if so, how? (e.g. repetition, contrasts, new material, different instruments, etc.)

Did the audience listen well?

Treasure Chest

Suggested Materials

Box containing a variety of objects with which you can make a sound (e.g. beads, comb, sandpaper, percussion instruments, etc.).

1. This activity is about careful listening, and using language to describe sound.

2. Position the box so that a sound can be made without the children seeing the object involved. Keeping the objects out of sight helps to promote a focus on the sound only. Asking the children to close their eyes when listening will also help.

3. Make a sound with one of the objects in the box. Ask the children to think of words to describe the sound made, for example:

    Sandpaper - *scratchy, rough, fuzzy*.

    Go through each sound making a collection of the words used.

4. Play the sounds to the children the next day/week. Can they match the sounds to their earlier descriptions of them? Can they add any more descriptive words?

Extension Activities

With older children this activity could be carried out in groups with the children recording their own descriptions. These descriptions can then be compared and the similarities and differences discussed.

Music Attainment Target: 2	English Attainment Target: 1
Main Focus: Listening	Main Focus: Vocabulary
Key Stage: 1	

Boo!

Suggested Listening

Once this activity is established, it may be accompanied by music with a strong beat (e.g. 'pop' or 'swing'). Can the children keep in time?

Children in a circle.

1. The children clap a constant pulse, e.g.

   1　2　3　4　1　2　3　4　1　2　3　4
   clap clap clap clap clap clap clap clap clap clap clap clap ....

2. Once the beat is steady, ask the children not to clap on '4', but instead make a silent gesture with their hands, e.g.

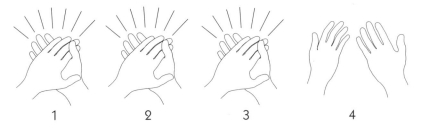

   1　　　　　2　　　　　3　　　　　4

3. The children now say 'Boo' on that silent beat, e.g. clap clap clap 'Boo', clap clap clap 'Boo', . . . etc.

4. Now try the same activity round the circle, everybody clapping and the children saying 'Boo' in turn.

Music Attainment Target: 1 & 2
Main Focus: Pulse
Key Stage: 1/2

English Attainment Target: 1
Main Focus: Vocal Participation

Colouring Names

Children in a circle.

1. Go round the circle, each child saying their name in turn.
2. Talk about the differences in our voices when we feel happy, and when we feel sad.
3. Now round the circle, the children say their names in a happy voice. Then repeat, using sad voices.
4. Gradually introduce other moods, e.g. scared, thoughtful, angry, excited, fed up, surprised, tired, etc.

Change the mood at various times round the circle.

Music Attainment Target: 1 & 2 Main Focus: Timbre Key Stage: 1/2	English Attainment Target: 1 Main Focus: Vocal Participation

Ants

Suggested Materials
Chart (see below). A selection of instruments.

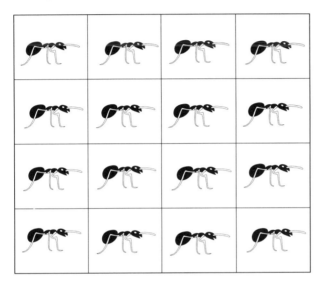

1. The children say 'Ant' as the teacher points rhythmically to each square. (Don't forget to indicate the speed before beginning.)
2. The children now clap the words instead of saying them.
3. Once the children can clap this rhythmically, try using instruments.
4. Now repeat the activity, removing one or two of the ants. The children say 'Ant' in their heads for these squares.

Music Attainment Target: 1 & 2
Main Focus: Pulse
Key Stage: 1/2

English Attainment Target: 1
Main Focus: Vocal Participation

Creepy Crawlies

Suggested Materials

Chart (see below). A selection of instruments.

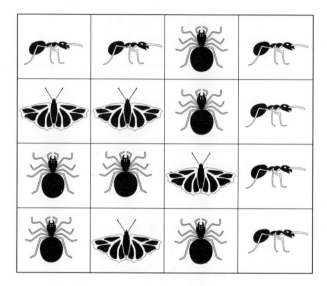

= Ant

= Spider

= Butterfly

1. As in the previous activity, but this time add words of two or more syllables to some of the squares, e.g. spiders, butterflies. Each word should be spoken within the same amount of time, i.e. one pulse.

   (Other words could be used relating to a theme, e.g. 'Colours', 'Explorers', 'Countries', etc.)

2. As for '**Ants**', develop by moving on to clapping words, and then playing on percussion.

Music Attainment Target: 1 & 2
Main Focus: Rhythm
Key Stage: 1/2

English Attainment Target: 4
Main Focus: Syllables

Connect

(See '**Boo**' first, page 9.) Children in a circle.

1. Instead of 'Boo' the children say the name of their favourite food.
2. Other alternatives might be colours, flowers, people, etc.
3. Once the children can maintain a sequence of four (three claps and a word), try other patterns, e.g.

Number
of beats:

3	clap	clap	*Chips*	clap	clap	*Pizza* . . .			
5	clap	clap	clap	clap	*Rose*	clap	clap	clap	clap *Tulip* . . .
7	clap	clap	clap	clap	clap	clap	*Red* . . .		
2	clap	*Peter*	clap	*Dharmesh* . . .					

(With odd-number patterns, be careful not to allow a gap between the word and the next clap.)

Extension Activities

Ask the children, in groups, to concentrate on performing one pattern together.

Ask the children to make the first clap of a pattern louder than the rest.

The groups perform to each other. Can the audience identify the pattern used?

Can two groups with different patterns perform simultaneously?

Music Attainment Target: 1 & 2
Main Focus: Pulse
Key Stage: 2

English Attainment Target: 1
Main Focus: Vocabulary

Associations

Follow on from '**Connect**'. Children in a circle.

1. Ask the first child to put any word they think of in the empty space.
   The next child must put in a related word, and so on round the circle, e.g.

   clap clap clap *Car*, clap clap clap *Wheel*, clap clap clap *Tyre*, clap clap clap *Sun* *.

   *If a child can think of no obvious connection, or says something unrelated, another member of the group can challenge. If the challenge is justified, the chain is broken and the game starts again.

2. The same activity can be played asking for pairs of opposites (e.g. night/day, good/bad); similar pairs (e.g. huge/big, shoe/boot); words with the same initial sounds (e.g. song/snake, dig/dog); or words beginning with consonant blends (e.g. blue/black/blow. . .).

Extension Activities

The above serve only as possible examples of categories. Choose any rule, according to the children's development and needs.

Remember to use a variety of number patterns. (See '**Connect**'.)

Music Attainment Target: 1 & 2 Main Focus: Rhythm Key Stage: 2	English Attainment Target: 1 Main Focus: Vocabulary

Name Tunes

Suggested Materials

Chime bars, glockenspiels, xylophones, set to a pentatonic scale (see Appendix).

Children should be divided into groups of four.

1. Ask the children, in their groups, to chant their own names rhythmically, and decide in which order they should be performed.
2. Now ask the groups to clap their sequences.
3. Give each group pitched instruments and ask them to work out a tune for their sequences, e.g.

    John   *Mar-jo-rie*   *Al-vin*   *Vik-esh*

4. Bring the groups together and listen to their tunes. Use other word rhythms, e.g. favourite food, names of vegetables, etc.

Extension Activities

Make a longer piece by putting the tunes of two or three groups into a short sequence.

Can two or three groups play their sequences together?

Music Attainment Target: 1 & 2 Main Focus: Rhythm and Melody Key Stage: 2	English Attainment Target: 4 Main Focus: Syllables

Sound Chance

Suggested Materials

Cards with a variety of instructions on them (see examples). A variety of percussion and other sound makers.

| A long, quiet sound. | A high sound. | Short, low sounds played quickly. |

| Short, low sounds played slowly and gradually becoming quicker. | Long sounds becoming quieter. |

(The instructions on the cards will depend on the age and ability of the children.)

1. The children sit in groups in a circle and each child in the group is dealt a card.
2. One by one each child shows their card and interprets the instruction on a sound maker. The group discusses whether the child has accurately interpreted the instruction.
3. Now the children order the cards to make a piece of music. They can use the cards more than once if they wish.

Extension Activities

Children can go on to write their own cards for another group to interpret. Useful vocabulary for the children to use on their cards:

       High – Low. Quickly – Slowly. Long – Short.
       Loud – Quiet. Solo – Group.

Music Attainment Target: 1
Main Focus: Exploring and Composing
Key Stage: 2

English Attainment Target: 1
Main Focus: Interpreting Instructions

Syllabox

Suggested Materials

Access to a variety of percussion. Prepared grid similar to the grid for **'Creepy Crawlies'** on a theme, e.g. Explorers. Blank grids for extension.

1. Following on from **'Creepy Crawlies'**, page 12, divide the children into groups, with each group responsible for one of the words in the grid, e.g.

    Group A = Hillary, Group B = Polo, Group C = Cook, etc.

2. The children follow the chart and say their words in the appropriate place. Having practised this, move on to performing by clapping, and then finally using instruments.

3. Divide the children into four groups, each playing one line repetitively. Can they keep together?

4. Explore other ways of structuring the piece, e.g. one group plays their line repetitively while other groups join in in turn, or play as a 'round', etc.

Extension Activities

The children may like to decide on a theme and produce their own pieces, to perform to the rest of the class. A supply of blank grids might be useful for this activity.

The children could further develop their pieces by considering grouping of percussion, inclusion of tuned percussion, and use of contrasts in playing, e.g. loud/quiet.

Music Attainment Target: 1 & 2 Main Focus: Rhythm Key Stage: 2	English Attainment Target: 4 Main Focus: Syllables

Music Critic

Suggested Materials

Tape-recorder. Tape with four short extracts of varied music (approx. 30 seconds to one minute each). Forms for the children to fill in (see opposite).

Suggested Listening

'Two Young Girls from Burundi', from *WOMAD 2* (WOM CD 003), 'The Bleating Lamb' from *Le Mystère des Voix Bulgares* (CAD603); extracts from *Passion-Sources* compiled by Peter Gabriel (RWCD1), Beethoven's Symphony No. 6, third movement, Mozart's Horn Concerto No. 4, last movement (Rondo), excerpts from Tchaikovsky's *Nutcracker Suite*, Saint-Saëns *Danse Macabre*, Mussorgsky's *Night on a Bare Mountain*, 'Portia' from *Tutu* by Miles Davies (9254902).

1. Play the tape to the children, asking them to sit very quietly with their eyes shut. Ask them to listen very carefully to the music, concentrating on what images and feelings are evoked by it.

2. Give out the forms to the children, with more or fewer categories depending on the age and experience of the children. Tell the children you will play the tape again, and this time they should fill in the form as they listen. Ask them to try and write down their immediate responses. (If necessary play the tape a third time so that all the children can finish writing their responses.)

3. Finally, play the tape once more, stopping after each extract for the children to give the pieces scores out of ten, according to their own preferences.

   (Do not expect specific answers from the children, e.g. 'The Swan' from *Carnival of the Animals* will not necessarily make them think of water, floating or white.)

Music	Colour	Place	Time	Feeling	Action	Score
1						
2						
3						
4						

4. Pick out common responses. What led to this? How did the composer achieve this? (For example, fast, busy music led to a picture of a party in the minds of some children.)
5. Responses could be tallied on a chart.
6. Note how often certain adjectives are used in describing the music.

Extension Activities

Play the tape again after a period of time (e.g. half a term), and see if responses differ. Alternatively, play it regularly for a short period of time and see if any children change preferences.

Music Attainment Target: 2
Main Focus: Appraising
Key Stage: 2

English Attainment Target: 1
Main Focus: Descriptive Vocabulary

Moving Words

Suggested Materials

A collection of words related to movement. Access to a variety of percussion instruments.

Suggested Word List

twirl, scamper, flit, bounce, slither, wiggle, wobble, whirl, leap, slide, shiver, drip, float, open, slide, glide, freeze, fluctuate, sink, drift, fall, drop, pause, collapse, explode, spread, grow, suspend.

1. Working in groups, the children are given one word to portray, using sound. Some words are easier than others; at first it may be helpful to discuss as a class the various possibilities, e.g.

    Sink soft, long sounds (xylophone played smoothly and slowly from top to bottom).
    Collapse sudden cymbal crash followed by a fast descending glissando on a glockenspiel, ending with a bang on a drum.

2. Having worked on their given word the groups perform to each other.
3. Groups can then be given a sequence of words as a stimulus for composition, e.g.

    scamper → freeze → whirl → leap → scamper.

Music Attainment Target: 1 Main Focus: Composing Key Stage: 2	English Attainment Target: 1 Main Focus: Vocabulary

Word Tunes

Suggested Materials

Xylophones, metallophones, glockenspiels and keyboards if available.

1. This activity is similar to the game in which as many words as possible are obtained from a master word. The scale most often used in western European music has seven notes - A B C D E F and G. Ask the children to look on the instruments and find these notes.

2. The children form a word from these letters (they can use the same letter more than once), then play their word on the instrument.

3. The children might like to see how many words they can make from these seven letters.

4. Once they have a list of words they could make a sentence incorporating two or more of the words, e.g.

    Beef and *cabbage* were served in the *café*
    Take a *cab*, there's no *fee* for your *baggage*.

5. The children can now try playing their sentences on instruments, playing the words underlined on tuned percussion, and those in between on untuned percussion (e.g. claves). Children decide how they will play these linking words (e.g. one tap for each letter, or one sound for each syllable).

Music Attainment Target: 1 & 2 Main Focus: Pitch Key Stage: 2	English Attainment Target: 4 Main Focus: Spelling

Pitch Words

Suggested Materials

Prepared pitch tracks (see below).

1. Talk to the children or read a passage from a book, keeping your voice on a monotone and avoiding inflection.
2. Discuss the difference between this and how you would normally talk/read out loud. What is missing? – the up and down movements of your voice (i.e. pitch). This is an essential ingredient in giving meaning and colour to our spoken language.
3. Look at particular words. Write 'pitch tracks' for them, e.g.

	fireworks	nursery rhymes	upstairs	downstairs
pitch tracks:	‾ _	‾ _ _	_ ‾	‾ _

NB It will become obvious that words can be said in a variety of ways depending on who is talking and in which context.

4. Have a pitch quiz. Choose six words. Decide beforehand how you are going to say them, and display their pitch tracks for the children to see. Ask the children to identify which pitch track matches the word you have said.

Extension Activities

Groups of children may then devise their own quiz for the rest of the class. They must take care that their vocal delivery matches the pitch tracks they have drawn for their words.

Music Attainment Target: 2
Main Focus: Pitch and Recording
Key Stage: 2

English Attainment Target: 1
Main Focus: Voice Colour

Pitch Sentences

Suggested Materials
Tuned percussion (e.g. xylophone, glockenspiel, chime bars).

1. From the previous activity it will be seen that words out of context can be pitched in many different ways. However, the pitch of a word placed in a sentence is often influenced by its context, e.g.

    (Following the pitch track with a finger while saying the sentence will help the children to 'feel' the differences in pitch.)

2. Sentences too can be said in different ways:

    How are you?   How are you?

3. Encourage the children to experiment by writing a sentence and then writing different pitch tracks for it. Which track works best and why?

Extension Activities
The children could transfer their pitch tracks onto tuned percussion and combine them end to end to make group tunes.

Music Attainment Target: 2 Main Focus: Recording Pitch Key Stage: 2	English Attainment Target: 1 Main Focus: Voice Colour

Voices Galore

Suggested Materials
Paper, marker pens.

1. The children, in groups, 'brainstorm' words which relate to different sounds that can be made by the human voice. The groups place the words they can think of randomly on a blank piece of paper, e.g.

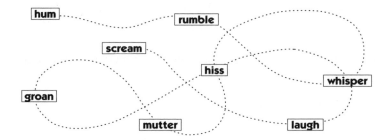

(Other possibilities include: roar, whistle, grumble, puff, gurgle, giggle, bleat, murmur, hiccup, buzz, howl, chortle, snigger, guffaw.)

2. Groups must now decide on a consistent vocal interpretation of each sound within the group. This will need much discussion and practice. They must also decide on the route they will take through the sounds. Groups may re-visit words as many times as they wish during their performance, as this will encourage the use of structuring devices such as sequencing and repetition.

3. Each group chooses a conductor who will help guide the group through their predetermined route in performance. Encourage the groups to work hard on the quality of their vocal sounds, aiming for clarity and accuracy in performance.

Music Attainment Target: 1 & 2 Main Focus: Exploring and Composing Key Stage: 2	English Attainment Target: 1 Main Focus: Vocabulary

Thesaurus

Suggested Materials
Paper to list words.

1. Having divided the children into groups, give each group one of the following words as a starting point:

    happiness, fear, tiny, sadness, huge, beautiful.

2. Ask each group to list the words that mean the same as, or are similar to, their given word.
3. Each group reports back to the class sharing the words they have found. Can anybody add any more words to any of the lists?
4. Ask each member of the group to pick out one word from their list and practise saying it in a way that reflects the overall 'feel' of their list, e.g.

    The 'happiness' group may choose to say their words brightly and fairly quickly.
    The 'fear' group may say their words slowly and quietly, with tremors in their voices!

5. Each group decides on an order, and builds up their words in layers to form a word piece, e.g.

Person 1	*glad*	*glad*	*glad*	*glad*	*glad*	*glad*
Person 2		*joyous*	*joyous*	*joyous*	*joyous*	
Person 3					*happiness*	*happiness*

6. Practice is needed for groups to fit words together well, and to sustain the overall mood of the piece. Groups can decide on their own ending; the 'happiness' group could burst into giggles, the 'tiny' group could get quieter and quieter.

Music Attainment Target: 1 & 2 Main Focus: Vocal Composing Key Stage: 2	English Attainment Target: 1 Main Focus: Vocabulary

Crack the Clue

Suggested Materials

Plenty of percussion and other sound makers. 'Clues' (see below).

Children in groups.

1. The children are attempting to 'solve' the problem of how to construct a piece of music. They receive one clue at a time, at random: one from category A, then one from B, and finally two from C, e.g.

A. Background	B. Melody/Rhythm	C. Effects
Constant, steady drumbeat throughout.	Must contain the rhythm of your name.	Cymbal crash.
Low, slow moaning sound.	Very slow repeating tune using G, A, C, and D.	Triangle.
Two chime bars (C and G) played together repetitively.	Five notes played quickly in sequence.	Two silences.
Glissando up and down on tuned percussion.	First line of the tune 'Three Blind Mice'	One loud drumbeat.
Repeated sequence of four sounds.	Two notes next door to each other played as a seesaw.	Claves played very quickly.
Repeated 'footsteps' on claves.		Whistle.
Cluster of any four notes played regularly throughout.		Owl hoot.
		Scream.
		Drum roll.

2. The children must work on each clue and prove to the teacher (Hercule Poirot!) that they have solved it, before receiving and incorporating the next clue into their music. Clue 'A' is played throughout, but the group must decide how and when to incorporate clues 'B' and 'C' into their piece.

Music Attainment Target: 1 & 2
Main Focus: Composing and Form
Key Stage: 2

English Attainment Target: 1
Main Focus: Interpreting Instructions

Appendix

Glossary

Crescendo	Getting louder.
Decrescendo	Getting quieter.
Drone	One or more notes maintained throughout a piece.
Dynamics	The gradations of volume in music.
Form	The order in which different ideas appear in a piece of music.
Improvisation	Composing spontaneously while performing.
Glissando	The process of moving from one note to another quickly, while playing all other notes in between.
Notation	The symbolic written representation of sound(s).
Ostinato	A rhythm or melody pattern repeated regularly during a piece of music (often as accompaniment).
Pitch	The perception of sounds as 'high' or 'low' in relation to each other. A woman's voice is usually higher in pitch than a man's.
Pulse	A repetitive, regular beat (sometimes silent), which can indicate the speed of a piece of music.
Rest	'Musical silence' – the absence of a sounding note or notes.
Rhythm	The pattern which long and short sounds and rests make when heard in sequence.
Rhythmic independence	The ability to maintain a rhythm against other rhythms.
Score	A written record of all the parts in a piece of music.
Sequencing	The ordering of sounds.
Timbre	The characteristics/colour of sound(s).
Volume	The loudness or quietness of sound/music.

Symbols

f	Loud
p	Quiet
$<$	Getting louder
$>$	Getting quieter

Pentatonic Scales

The notes on tuned percussion should be arranged with long bars to the left, getting increasingly smaller to the right-hand side, and in alphabetical order. Most (but not all) start with 'C'.

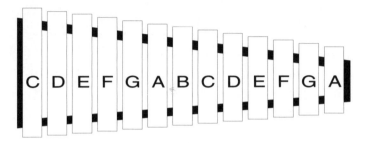

By removing any note 'B' and any note 'F', it is possible to have a five-note scale, called 'Pentatonic' (Penta = five). This should leave a sequence of C D E G A.

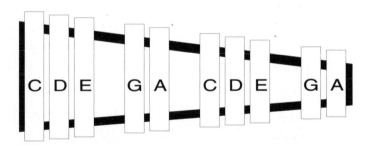

A pentatonic scale is useful for improvising melodies, both solo and in group work.

Occasionally instruments will come with notes called 'sharps' (with a ♯ after the letter), and 'flats' (with a ♭ after the letter), e.g. C♯ E♭ F♯ G♯ B♭. By using only these notes, it is again possible to create a pentatonic scale. This same scale can be found by just using the black notes on a piano or keyboard. Use this scale if most of the notes on your tuned percussion are sharps and flats.